T0080387

GO CAMPING!

by
Heather Bode

Published by Capstone Press, an imprint of Capstone
1710 Roe Crest Drive, North Mankato, Minnesota 56003
capstonepub.com

**Library of Congress Cataloging-in-Publication Data is available on
the Library of Congress website.**
ISBN 9781666345599 (hardcover)
ISBN 9781666345605 (paperback)
ISBN 9781666345612 (eBook PDF)

Summary: Describes the types of camping, the supplies campers
need, and the activities campers can participate in outdoors.

Image Credits
Getty Images: AleksandarNakic, 29, Ariel Skelley, 5, Imgorthand,
6, 11, 23, Jordan Siemens, 8, Klaus Tiedge, 13, SrdjanPav, 10;
Shutterstock: Amelia Martin, 20, Amorn Suriyan, 28, anatoliy_gleb,
18, AnnaStills, 14, BalanceFormCreative, 27 (top), David Pereiras, 15,
Dmitry Naumov, 19, Dragon Images, 17, Max Topchii, 25, Monkey
Business Images, 1, Cover, nulinukas, 7, Tupungato, 22, Valeriia
Soloveva, 27 (leaf, pine cone), VectorShow, 27 (wood piles), Virrage
Images, 9, yui, 21

Editorial Credits
Editor: Erika L. Shores; Designer: Dina Her; Media Researchers:
Jo Miller and Pam Mitsakos; Production Specialist: Tori Abraham

Table of Contents

Words in **bold** are in the glossary.

Chapter 1

CAMPING BY THE NUMBERS

You gaze up at the sky. The fire crackles. Everyone jokes about the day's events. It must be close to bedtime. But time does not matter here. You pull a sticky marshmallow off your roasting stick and bite into it. Dessert before bedtime? Why not? This is camping.

In 2020, 48 million households went camping. Out of that number, 10 million groups were first-time campers. On average, a person takes their first camping trip at age 10. Are you around that age? Then perhaps it is time for you to go camping!

Camping is an outdoor activity that people of all ages take part in.

Chapter 2

CAMPING CATEGORIES

There is a type of camping for everyone. Learn about the different camping categories to find the right fit for you.

Are you testing out new camping equipment? Backyard camping provides practice before heading out to campgrounds. Backyard camping is also perfect for first-time campers. You will be close to a bathroom and kitchen. You can run inside if it rains.

Backyard camping combines the fun of camping with the convenience of being at home.

Car camping, or tent camping, happens at campgrounds. You pay a **fee**. The campground gives you a place to park your car and **pitch** a tent. This is your campsite. Campgrounds may have showers, **outhouses** or bathrooms, **fire rings**, and picnic tables.

Campsites can be close together at some campgrounds.

Car Camping History

Car camping first became popular about 100 years ago, as cars became widely available. People attached a canvas roof (tent) to the side of the car and slept alongside the road or in farmers' fields. Famous people like Thomas Edison and Henry Ford and many American presidents went camping. This helped car camping grow in popularity.

Backpacks made to carry camping gear are large, lightweight, and have many padded straps.

Backpacking is the hardest way to camp. It means you must hike to your campsite. You carry all your supplies on your back. It is important to keep the weight of your backpack as light as possible. You must bring along food, shelter, and clothing.

Campers and recreational vehicles (RVs) are another way to camp. They have beds, give more weather protection, and may have bathrooms. Some people use their RVs to go **boondocking**. This is free camping on public lands outside of campgrounds. Sometimes you may even see boondocking done in store parking lots.

Camping using recreational vehicles means you can bring along a table and chairs.

FACT

Today, some people still camp like they did 100 years ago. They use tents to camp on public land that is not set aside as campgrounds or parks. This is called **dispersed** camping.

Most people camp in the summer. But camping can be done in any season, even in winter. Winter camping requires special clothes, shelter, and sleeping gear. Campgrounds may not have water or open bathrooms. But you will also not have any bugs!

No matter what kind of camping you do, treat the outdoors with respect. Only camp on surfaces that will not damage plants and grasses. Pick up any trash. Be careful with fire. Together, everyone can help protect the natural world.

A group learns how to make a fire during a winter camping trip.

Chapter 3

GETTING THE GOODS

When you go camping, you must bring along everything you need. It is important to have the right supplies.

Being outside will make you hungry. You may eat twice as much as you do at home. Food will help fuel you for the day's activities. Muffins, bagels, hard-boiled eggs, and bananas are quick breakfasts. If you have more time, oatmeal, eggs, and pancakes taste great on a chilly morning.

For lunch, sandwiches along with apples, veggies, and chips can be taken with you on a hike. Bring snacks too. Pack granola bars, trail mix, nuts, and dried fruit in your backpack.

Dinner can be hot dogs or canned stew. You may even buy freeze-dried meals. Add boiling water, wait a few minutes, open the bag, and eat. Does this sound funny? It is how astronauts eat in space!

Some people bring along their own small grills
to cook on while camping.

Bring clothing that can be layered. You may need a hat and jacket in the morning when it is cooler.

Clothing needed for camping depends on the weather forecast, the time of year, and the **altitude** of your campsite. As altitude increases, temperature decreases.

Use weather forecasts to help you plan. Will it be very warm? Bring sandals and shorts. Are you camping in the fall? Bring jackets and long pants. Are you staying in the mountains? Bring a winter hat, a warm coat, and wool socks.

If you are using a tent, make sure it is **waterproof**, lightweight, and easy to put together. Bring a hammer to pound in the tent stakes.

You may want to bring along a few other supplies. **Binoculars** are great for animal watching. Headlamps make nighttime trips to the bathroom much easier. Garden gloves are useful when arranging firewood. Nobody wants painful slivers in their hands.

You can bring a lantern to use when it's dark. Binoculars are useful for spotting birds and other wildlife.

Chapter 4

CAMPING FUN AND GAMES

Some people go camping just to relax. Others go for serious outdoor adventure.

Camping close to a lake means you can go fishing, swimming, or boating. There may be hiking trails and ranger talks where you can learn about local plant and animal life. If a campground is paved, bikes and scooters are fun ways to explore the area. If you enjoy art, sketch a tree from different points of views.

Create your own games. Make a list of items to find for a scavenger hunt. Tour the campground to vote on the best campsite. Look at license plates to find where other campers came from.

You can catch your dinner if your campsite is near a lake or river.

FACT

The average child only spends about 4 to 7 minutes outside each day.

Camping gives you the opportunity to view the night sky.

The farther you travel from a city, the brighter the stars become. Take time to do some stargazing. Grab binoculars to get a better look at what's in the night sky. Check out the moon. You can use star charts to help identify stars and planets. There are apps you can download too. Use them to find and name **constellations**.

Another fun nighttime idea is to use your tent to create shadow puppet shows. One person stands outside the tent with a flashlight. This person uses hands or objects to make "puppets." The audience watches from inside the tent.

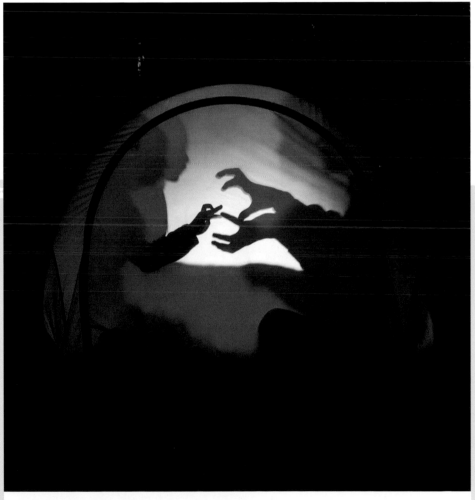

Use your hands and a flashlight to make shadow puppets.

Chapter 5

BE A SAFETY SUPERSTAR

Being outside all day comes with dangers. Stay safe by following some important tips.

Campgrounds post rules to keep you safe. Cars and campers need to follow low speed limits. Always watch for moving vehicles when you walk or ride bike. Campgrounds also have quiet hours. This time allows people to sleep. Remember that tent walls are not your bedroom walls. Even if you think you are being quiet, your neighbors might not agree.

Follow campground rules to be a safe and courteous camper.

**Rocks can serve as a fire ring to keep
a campfire from spreading.**

Fires must be constantly watched. Use a fire ring
or rocks to keep the fire contained. Make sure there
are no low-hanging branches above your campfire.
Always have water nearby. Remove anything that
people might trip over near the fire.

Campground critters love to investigate your campsite. Do not leave food or garbage out. Put food inside your car, camper, or a **food locker**. If you are backpacking, tie food and garbage up in a tree.

There will be bugs too. Insect **repellent**, hats, and long-sleeved clothes help protect you from bites.

A food locker keeps your food safe from wildlife.

Use insect repellent to keep bugs away while you're outdoors.

You need a clean water supply. Most campgrounds provide water. Never drink out of lakes and streams unless you filter, or clean, the water.

If you plan on swimming, many campground swim areas do not have lifeguards. Know your abilities and stay with your group. Make sure an adult is nearby. When in doubt, wear a life jacket.

Chapter 6

THE PITCH AND PACK PRO

Camping is a lot of work. The more you help, the better the experience will be for your family.

BEFORE YOU GO

- ☑ Practice setting up the tent.
- ☑ Use maps to decide where you will camp.
- ☑ Make a checklist of supplies.
- ☑ Pack your clothes.
- ☑ Gather supplies and bring them to the vehicle.
- ☑ Talk about how each person can be a responsible camper:
    - ☑ Pick up trash.
    - ☑ Stay on trails. No shortcuts!
    - ☑ Do not feed wild animals.
    - ☑ Do not collect natural objects such as wildflowers, rocks, or seashells.

You'll use ropes and stakes to keep your tent
attached to the ground.

WHEN YOU REACH YOUR CAMPSITE

- ☑ Read the campground rules.
- ☑ Locate the water and bathrooms.
- ☑ Unpack the vehicle.
- ☑ Choose a flat spot for your tent or camper.
- ☑ Clear the area of rocks.
- ☑ Set up the tent if you have one.
- ☑ Put sleeping bags and clothing in the right spots.
- ☑ Reread the campground rules. Some campgrounds do not let you gather wood because it is harmful to the environment to remove it. In that case, buy wood from the campground.
- ☑ If gathering wood is allowed, look for dry wood that is already lying on the ground.
- ☑ Use garden gloves to sort wood from smallest to largest. ONLY ADULTS start the fire!

Setting up the tent

Firewood

To build a campfire, you need wood in different sizes.

- ☑ tinder (pine cones, dried leaves, dried grasses, or newspaper)
- ☑ kindling (tiny sticks about the size of pencils)
- ☑ big sticks (as thick as your arm)
- ☑ logs

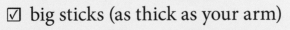

WHEN IT IS TIME TO LEAVE

☑ Pack up clothes and sleeping bags.

☑ Collapse and pack the tent if you have one.

☑ Clean up all of your garbage.

☑ Help unpack the vehicle when you get home.

You are a big influence on your family. Be sure to tell them what a great time you had. If you enjoyed camping, your family will be more likely to do it again. See you at the campground!

Pick up trash before you leave for home.

Packing up the campsite

GLOSSARY

altitude (AL-ti-tood)—how high an object is above sea level

binoculars (buh-NAH-kyuh-luhrz)—a tool that makes faraway objects look closer

boondocking (BOON-dock-ing)—using an RV and camping for free on public lands

constellation (kahn-stuh-LAY-shuhn)—a group of stars that forms a shape

dispersed (dis-PURSD)—spread out

fee (FEE)—a payment in exchange for a service

fire ring (FYR RING)—a metal or stone ring used to contain a fire

food locker (FOOD LOCK-ur)—a metal container provided by the campground in which you can store food

outhouse (OUT-hous)—a toilet without plumbing

pitch (PICH)—to set up and fix firmly in place

repellent (ri-PEL-uhnt)—a substance applied to the skin and clothes that is used to keep insects away

waterproof (WAH-tur-proof)—able to keep water out

READ MORE

Kingston, Seth. *Camping.* New York: PowerKids Press, 2022.

Ogintz, Eileen. *The Kid's Guide to Camping.* Lanham, MD: Falcon Guides, 2021.

Towell, Colin. *Survival!: A Step-by-Step Guide to Camping and Outdoor Skills.* New York: DK Publishing, 2019.

INTERNET SITES

Find a Campground
nps.gov/subjects/camping/campground.htm

The Great American Campout
nwf.org/Great-American-Campout/About

Leave No Trace Center for Outdoor Ethics
lnt.org/courses/PEAKOnline2020_HTML5/

INDEX

ABOUT THE AUTHOR

Heather Bode is an elementary educator and author. She loves writing nonfiction she knows will be high-interest material for her students. Heather lives in Helena, Montana.